Spiraling

Eve Hufnagel Cone

BOMBSHELTER PRESS
Los Angeles / 2012

Copyright © 2012 Eve Hufnagel Cone
All rights reserved

Other than brief quotations in a review, no part of this book may be reproduced without written permission of the publisher or copyright holder.

ISBN: 978-0-941017-95-4

Bombshelter Press
www.bombshelterpress.com
books@bombshelterpress.com
PO Box 481266 Bicentennial Station
Los Angeles, California 90048 USA

Printed in the United States of America

Front cover photo: Corinna Jones
Author photo: John Iverson
Proof reading: Michaelann & Rob Dimitrijevich

Layout & design: Alan Berman

Contents

Poetry

One Rose	9
The Longer I Walk	10
The Picnic	11
Waves and War	12
At What Age	14
The Wildness	15
The Gift Exchange	16
Toned Up	18
The Perfect White Towel	20
More Varieties of Spiritual Experience	21
Harvest Moon	22
I Know	23
The Daniel Poem	25
Feeding the Python	28
Bringing Home the Buddha	29
Breaking the Law	31
Susie's Painting	32
These Few Things	33
Alleluia, Lord Have Mercy	35
Another Leap	36
After the Wildfire	37
At the Window	38
Separate Lives	39
Collision Tears	40
Laundry and Death	41
Bleeding Time	43
What Is Tall and Spews Marbles	44
Silence	45
The Dead Man	46
The Familiar Red	49
Weird Waltzing	51

Motion

Zanzibar	55
Oatmeal	57
Divine Intervention	59
Everyone Should Have a Chance	61
Effortless	63
Push, Glide, Glide	65
The Toy Shop	66
Large Talents	67
Country Culture	69
Full Circle	71
Topanga	76
And Then One Day	78

Spiraling

Poetry

One Rose

I'm a one-rose kind of person.
A single rose holds all I can handle
    of life, beauty, sadness, love.
I'm a single, one-moment type person:
    this moment, a finished product,
        all there is, not a trial run.
I paint a picture, it's finished, not
    in process; I bake oatmeal cookies,
    finished, all clear.

"You never have anything in process,"
    he said, after we met.
But single moments are all I can take,
    sometimes more than I can take.
Maybe I learned some of this
        from my father,
    a one-moment, one-is-enough
    kind of person, or maybe from the convent,
        one pair of shoes, one black habit,
        one single bed, one small desk,
        one community.
My favorite things come in ones:
    one moon, one sun, one ocean,
    one Venus, one Mars, one You.
While some search for
        more and more
I look for less and less.
I do admire people who build strong,
    sound buildings, and dig deep wells
        and crave diamonds and shoes,
    more couches, more art and music,
        more homes.
I admire people who sink their hands
    day after day, year after year, to shape
        and process and prepare for their
    breath-taking final This-is-it!
A dozen roses could take me
        straight to insanity.

The Longer I Walk

I walk in the middle of the Great Depression
    my father and mother nursing
        too many babies
in the tornado family in Oklahoma
    all of us lying on the front porch
      'til things cool down on hot August
        nights watching the stars
to Catholic schools, dodging Monsignor
    pinching my cheeks during hop-scotch
    kingdom-come catechism classes
to the wasteland of adolescence and the
    bronzing of my older brothers, sweet-
    talking me out of the house and onto the
        road to boarding school, cool
          shelter from beer cans and dates and
            lightning strikes
to the windows of college, and teaching down
        long black dresses and coifs
    covering blond hair and body
        out of sight out of mind
to the freedom lands of hippo lakes
        and hyena villages
    walking the rainy season of Africa
    to the death of my father and the death of my
    mother and the death of old lovers
    whose names I can't right now remember
up to Topanga raising my son without a father
to the top of the steep hill to the rock with a view
        where eagles fly, down backs my strong
        hands healing massage route
through the over and over mantra streets of L.A.
    past my bedroom mirror of surface veins
        and wrinkled dreams.
        The longer I walk the more I become.

The Picnic

The picnic table on the windy hilltop is not pretty.

The ketchup bottle, the cardboard containers
   of Knudsen's potato salad and cole slaw
     on the wooden table, the buns, the potato chips,
       the summer sun, the wind, the dust,
           the barren hills.

I try to anchor parts
  of the white paper table cover.
My blond hair sweeps up in the wind
  as I bend over a plate, a mix of sand and sun
     and wind,
        and I am little more.
Why am I alone at this table?
It's a picnic. Why is everyone still hiking?

Does it matter that I'm here in my
  blue sweatshirt and red shorts,
my thoughts, like the rolling hills behind me,
  barren, blowing away.
My two hands against a dry wind sweeping
  from the ocean up the hillside.

I am the woman with the wind and the sand
and the sun, flying hair and sun-burned legs,
arms reaching out and torso bent over
               the picnic table.

Waves and War

It was a simple thing.
I was driving down Highway 101
       just south of San Francisco.
I came upon a military
       transport truck full of soldiers.
As I came close to pass, I took off
       my sunglasses and leaned
     forward a little to smile and wave.
  The soldiers leaned in reflex towards me
    and waved, all smiles and arms.

Then I remembered about wartime and
       I cried.
I was only six when all the young
       men left.
It was quiet after that; things changed,
   and things were missing, like shoes
     and tires and gasoline, and sugar,
             especially sugar,
    All the young men gone and no sugar.
It would have been so much easier to have the
   young men gone if we had
           had some sugar.

It was a heavy time, too, and dark.
My older sisters had lovers in the war.
I remember that Lucy
   wore the same purple and white shorts
      every day one summer.
She spent a lot of time at the piano
      playing "As Time Goes By" and
         "Moonlight Cocktails"... couple
     a jiggers of moonlight and add a star...
Sometimes we sang with her.

My other sister Helen spent
   a lot of time ironing, with the radio
next to her tuned to the latest invasion.

      She wrote letters every day to Tom.
I watched her seal them
           with red lipstick kisses.

It was a bad time for mothers, too.
        I noticed them.
On Sunday, Louise, who lost her son Bobby,
    would shuffle down the aisle of Holy
       Trinity Church and genuflect.
As she turned to go into the pew,
    I would see that she had
shriveled a little more with her grief.

And some of the young wives went
    mad and had to have electroshock
        treatments.
For us kids, it was mostly
    deprivation, but we saved dimes
       on those coin cards to help
          the War.

By the time I reached Montecito on the 101,
    I got off the freeway for a cappuccino,
        with sugar,
    a little refreshment after the ride
      from San Francisco
         on a memorable California day.

At What Age

At what age does a woman start
tending outdoor plastic flowers?
Every day I drive the last mile home
and make the last sharp left turn up
up the hill and see the familiar grey-haired
small woman caressing
her plastic flower displays.

Close to the 4th of July
everything is red, white and blue daisies
and small American flags.
For spring there are pots of plastic tulips
and jonquils and lilies with matching
yellow, pink and blue banners.
For fall there are golden browns
and deep yellows, five pots of warm-colored flowers,
topped with flowered flags and an orange pumpkin.

At what age does a woman start tending
plastic flowers?
My older sister said she put plastic flowers
on our parents' graves this year.

The Wildness

As a child I wanted to be close to
        wild animals.
I coaxed the squirrel into
    my grandfather's abandoned
        blacksmith shop.
The squirrel wandered in
        but stayed only a day.
Then came a feral cat near the old well.
I sat very still, barely breathing, as it
        came so close
    hoping it could be tamed, that the
        wildness would leave.
But the wildness didn't leave and the
    cat and the squirrel left
            as they had come.
Now you have gone, too, though I lay very
        still, barely breathing,
    as you came so close, hoping you
        would stay, near the well,
    that your wildness would leave.

The Gift Exchange

I see you bent over the large bread pan, Mom.
Your strong arms knead twenty loaves of bread a week.
And I know every bed in our home is covered
with blankets and quilts you've made yourself.
You hold geese between your legs, their wings
pinned with one arm, while you pluck down
from their breasts for our pillows.

Your breasts ... I can't imagine you nursing
eleven children from those breasts I've never seen.
And my breasts at thirteen? Are you so milked
that breasts are breasts, just breasts.
We don't talk about breasts.

Three times a day our family sits at the linen-covered
table in our farm house, every bite of food
something your hands have touched long before
it reaches the table, but you never touched
me.

You nurture the seeds in the garden
and there are all those seeds of children in you.

I bleed more from my heart than my vagina
when you point to the rags on the shelf
without a word on womanhood.

The hours you cook, wash, iron, clean, can, bake,
make soap, sew—every dress I wear is designed
by you. I feel you've stitched the skin I wear.

I haven't gone near you in years, not really since 16.
After three decades, I have something to say.

There's a strong man walking around inside you.
I was fed at the breast of a man, clothed,
sheltered by a man, a wonderful man.
The woman was not there.

And there's more. There's a soft woman
walking around in this angular, masculine
body of mine. I don't know
what to do with the man on the outside of me.

I see everyone else still reach to you
for the woman who is not there.
Not I. I choose to make my peace
with this exchange.

I need your man's heart to survive.
You need my woman's heart to die.

Toned Up

All the passion was gone
from my life the day
I decided to see Wayne,
the sound healing therapist.
Wayne does electronic analysis
of the speaking voice which shows balances
and imbalanced in the body.

I had a session with Wayne
and came home with
a graph of my voice, and
six personalized toning tapes at $20 each.

"Way out of balance," Wayne said,
after an hour of electronic analysis.
He showed me my graph, the heavy
blue and red lines
indicating my right-brain side.

"Your intuitive side is on heavy overload;
this could even cause
digestive problems," he said.

Then, surely as night follows day,
I saw on the other side of the graph
a few pale pink marks on the almost
empty left-brain side.
The tones missing: C, A, A#, Bb, B, G, G#.
I saw the left-brain side needed
immediate attention, so as soon as I got home
I started playing my left-brain personalized
toning tapes to fill in that side;
the wha-wha-wha repetition of the tones,
not exactly like the soft flute music
I usually listened to.

For ten days I played the tapes, still
not sure how any of this really works.
(I'm keeping an eye on my cat)
The A# tape in the background is starting
to sound a lot like the spa motor next door.
I noticed yesterday's B tape had a tone
matching the clothes dryer.
I'm looking forward to the arrival of the
garbage truck tomorrow morning; the G# of
all that crashing, slamming of metal
against metal on the dumpster.

Wonderful world of spa motors clothes dryers
garbage trucks screaming babies and
barking dogs jack hammers banging garage doors,
clanking, screaming, banging tones
giving back my lost left brain,
and my toned, passionate life.

The Perfect White Towel

On a day when everyone else
  is at work, I love driving down the coast.
Today the clouds are creamy and dragony,
   the waves are white hats, the hillsides
    gardens of yellow clover and fuchsia
    against fresh green grass.
Today I'm a mesmerized driver who might
  be honked through green lights.
It's that kind of perfect day.

The sign says Oxnard, and I stop
  at a service station that says only
    Self-Serve.
I check the oil and can't get a read.
I stick the stick in, pull it out, stick it in,
    pull it out: no reading.

I ask for help from a heavy man
  who tells me I'm getting no reading
  because I've no oil, two quarts low.
How can that be, I ask, where does it go?

Well, there's the burn-off, he says,
  always, the burn-off.

A man with a shriveled leg fills my
  gas tank at the Self-Serve pump; he
  notices the grease on my hands
    and takes me to the mechanics' sink in back.
He hands me a blue bottle of grease-
   removing soap, then unlocks a tall metal cabinet,
    and lifts a perfect white towel for my hands.

Now I turn back to the drive toward home.

It's the burn-off, always the burn-off.
  and a perfect white towel
            for my hands.

More Varieties of Spiritual Experience

Nikki comes running out to my car
    as I drive up to his home for our appointment.
    "Wait 'til we get inside!"
        (He gives me that grin.)

Once I get inside the door with my massage
    table and bag, he sticks out his
    tongue to show me his latest body piercing.
I let out something between a gasp and a scream,
        which is all he really wants.

I move on to setting up the massage table
    in the usual place, between the white marble
    fireplace and the life-sized wooden sculpture
        of a baby giraffe wearing a saddle.

All set for the massage, I look down on
    Nikki's fully-tattooed torso and arms.
A large tattooed sun in the middle
        of his back smiles up at me;
I smile back and spread the sun's face with oil.
"Shopping Cart Jesus" plays in the background.

I take a deep breath and move into the massage—
        Not the convent in Kansas anymore.

Harvest Moon

Deep Throat Carnival
    open   wounds
                let in light
   oven brightness
and ocean seams

  stomach ulcers catch cold with Barbara

  no matter about tinsel turner

Your smile steals noodles of canisters
     off the shelf

Amen   Amen

Enough of this struggle

      Shine

Shine   on

    harvest moon

I Know

Marcel is dead.

If only I could have made amends to him
    for the question I didn't answer.

Marcel Montecino.
His mystery novel in there and white jacket
    jumps out from my bookcase shelf.

Right there, *SACRED HEART*, in white letters
    against a large black crucifix, the
    novel I still haven't read after four years.

That evening as he and I sat at the head table
    of the drug and alcohol panel,
Marcel, in front of everyone, decides to bring
    me up to date on his latest 1920s novel about
    a Mexican priest and a nun who fall in love.

Marcel leans towards me in a low voice,
"They are ready to make love,
    can you describe her underwear for me?"

I smooth my hair behind my ear and whisper,
    "I don't know what kind of underwear nuns wear."

He knows that a few months prior
    I had described for him the things nuns wear:
    black-draped veils, white coifs and bonnets.

Now I bite my lip. I almost say: "It's a white
    lace teddy, like the ones from Victoria's Secret."
But tonight I don't ruin Marcel's search for the truth,
    not at this moment with his soft, low voice posing
        the historical novelist's question.

I observe the disappointment on Marcel's face.
    He relaxes into his straight-backed chair,
        sips his coffee and whispers,
      "I guess I'll have to do more research."

I know Marcel is a thorough researcher;
    he'll comb Mexico and the Southwest
    for a single truth, even down to the nun's underwear.

Now Marcel is dead. Cancer.

If only I could make amends
    for the question I didn't answer.
        I knew the answer.

The Daniel Poem

I need a poem today
        as much as I've needed anything.
I call Dutton's, they can't help, and
Deep River Book Store says: "Poem? What's
    a poem? I don't know poems, send a list."

So, I get in my car and swing
        through Santa Monica and down
            into the soul of Venice to
                    Beyond Baroque.
The bookstore attendant is new to LA,
    and can't help; he hands me a Bill Knott
        book of poems, but Bill Knott
            is not what I need.

So, for sentimental reasons, I drive two blocks
    up the alleyway to the small old house
        on Amoroso Court where I lived
            20 years ago.
I see the antique-blue cracked back door and
    the driveway just large enough for
                my VW Beetle.
And, I see the small garage, I think about
        young Daniel, my former neighbor
                (gaunt as Van Gogh)
    who lived in that tiny space and played
    Bach and Chopin all day,
            his enormous piano music
floating through the cracks and keyholes
        and the wide, unsealed spaces
        of our old Venice neighborhood homes.

                    And I recalled that hot humid August night.
At 3:00 A.M. I heard a rustling sound;
            I went from the bedroom to the kitchen
                        to check it out.
        There, before me, in the dim reflected light,
                        a large leg
        arched over the kitchen window sill and a shoulder
                leaned into the window shade.
I gasped and gulped an in-breath, gasped and gulped again,
            and with that the large form backed out
                                the window into the night.
I ran to the window
        leaning into my fiercest scream; a sound that
                did not represent anything human.
                            I tried again.
With that young Daniel roared
            out of the garage with his best Tarzan cry
                and flew to my kitchen door.
There we stood in the middle of the kitchen,
                shaken and scared.

I explained the rustling sound, the shade,
            the shoulder leaning in,
                the foot almost touching the floor.
He told about my screams, his thoughts
                of an attack.
        For ten minutes we worked for calm and composure.

Then we saw:
        Neither of us was wearing clothes.
                He looked and I looked.
                        Daniel!

Just then five police officers arrived in response to
    a neighborhood call, and Daniel and I
                        made a run for our clothes.

For weeks afterwards Daniel lingered close
    to check on my safety and to be there
        " ... in case there was anything else
        I had in mind."
  But I was a single-minded single parent
      who didn't have anything else in mind.

Today, twenty years later
      at 812 Amoroso Court I wonder
  about young Daniel, his Chopin and Bach,
    and whatever else he has in mind.

Feeding the Python

Today I feed my son's python;
I don't know how others feed pythons
    or even if there is a proper way
        to feed a python,
I only know how I feed our python.
    I take the python from his cage;
        carry him, always coiled, into
    my son's shower, where I have placed a
        large Nordstrom's shopping bag.
I put the python in the bag in the shower stall.
      Then, and this is the part
            I loathe,
      I open a small brown box containing
        a cute white feeder mouse.
    I drop the sweet mouse onto
          the coiled snake in the bag;
I slam the shower door and rush away
    from the room, but never fast enough
        to have missed hearing that
          rustling snap in the paper bag
(which I always try to imagine I haven't heard).

This morning after dropping the feeder mouse,
      I grab my wallet and head
            up the street to the supermarket.
I buy fish and chicken, bread and broccoli;
    and then, with my arms coiled round my bags,
        I slither down the street
                    back home again.

Bringing Home the Buddha

And now I have a Buddha on my balcony.

I had not thought of having a Buddha,
    but it feels right to look out from my living room
        and see the Buddha sitting with his half-smile,
holding a rose in the right hand near his heart
    and a dome-shaped, seven-pointed
        offering dish in his left hand resting on his knee.

I was driving up Pacific Coast Highway
    when I spotted the granite Buddha
        high on the edge of the nursery roof.
The roof was lined with large pottery pots
    and in the center of the line was a Buddha
           facing the ocean.

At that moment I knew I wanted that Buddha.

After my ocean-front drive, I stopped at sundown
    to get the Buddha, and I bought a bright orange
        cactus as my first Buddha offering.
The Vietnamese nurseryman took the Buddha,
    placed it in the passenger seat of my VW,
        then pressed the cactus next to it.

"You are Eve, of course," he said, closing the door.

I drove home with the smiling granite Buddha next to me.
As luck would have it, my teen-aged son had stopped by
        and was lounging in the living room.
Together we returned to the garage and I held the doors
    while my son carried the large granite Buddha
        like a baby in his arms.

We walked in silence upstairs from the garage
        to the condominium balcony.

He placed the Buddha among the plants.
I placed the orange cactus beside the Buddha's left knee.

My son and the Buddha—their quiet smiles,
    their patient waiting, their granite grace.

My son is gone.
A smiling Buddha sits on my balcony.

Breaking the Law

Every day I break the law.
Three or four times a day I break the law.
"Massaging buttocks is breaking the law,"
Marilyn said, as she massaged my buttocks.

"That's weird, isn't it," I say, feeling her strong hands
(strong as mine) kneading my buttocks. "So good."

Here I am every day with people whose tired bodies
        lie on my massage table.

Jeff lay like an angel on the massage table.
I gave him a massage, loosening the muscles of his back.

"I sit in front of a computer," he says,
"twelve to fourteen hours a day.
"This week my back began to spasm every time
        I picked up the mouse."

"I know," I say, and I stop there, remembering
        my chalk dust days in the classroom.

    Every day I break the law.

Gus calls, asking for just a half hour, if I don't have
an hour. "I can't lie on my back," he says.
I give him one of my pregnant woman massages.
"So much better," he says, "the pain was taking my breath away."

Now I offer my own body to my slant board;
        blood rushes to my head;
I swing my legs and hips in scissor exercises.

So many bodies, some better than others,
I now favor the irregular, all the scars and moles
and creases and folds. Beautiful irregularities I call them.
        Enough of Playboy Centerfolds
        lamonized upon my table.

Susie's Painting

In a dim parking lot
      she opens the trunk of her car
   and takes out her painting
      of a wedding party,
  a wedding party winding
through a spring pasture.

We each hold an edge
  of the picture
      and smile at the scene.
And then,
     like some of our dreams,
  we close it in the trunk again.

These Few Things

I'm looking at a large jawbone with teeth
    lying on the floor beside a Kenyan drum
    in a corner of my living room in Santa Monica.

Above the drum is a pastel picture of Running
    Horse, my Indian guide, in a feathered headdress
    with leather strips dangling over his ears.

Across the front of the picture of Running Horse
    I've draped a strand of amethyst quartz beads, my gift.
    I remember the precise day I received each item.

The deer jawbone with the teeth was a gift
    from my son Michael and his friend Nicky
    after their exploration in Topanga State Park
        when they were eight years old.

The picture of Running Horse, a pastel, was
    drawn by a man who told me my secrets
        while he drew.

On the opposite side of the room,
    between a Dream Catcher and a suede pouch
    of feathers, are sage and dried flowers.

Above a couple of small drums is a pastel
    of my son's Indian guide, Golden Eagle.

The rest of the living room is like any ordinary
    room except for the eight large pink and lavender
        corals and sea shells and the large Tibetan calendar.

I suppose the little pouches of runes and animal cards
    are not in every living room, and maybe not the
        Tibetan bowl or the rain stick above the fireplace,
           or the large chunks of amethyst quartz,
        and the abalone shells or the bundles of sage
        with feathers in the ceramic pot
                      in front of the fireplace.

Other than that, it's an ordinary living room:
    a couch, a chair, a coffee table and a book shelf.

I forgot to mention a small icon of the Black Madonna,
            Our Lady of Vladimir.
I kept her hidden for twenty-seven years in a dark corner
    of the closet; recently she's come out.

Also, I forgot to mention the rosary beads I keep hidden
    in a red box in the bottom drawer of the wall unit.
    They are in memory of my father who used them
    at Mass rather than follow the Latin Sunday Missal.

I'm not a person who collects treasures, but I do have a
    cardboard box of old photographs and letters
    and some poems from a former student,
    Mike Tharp, during the war in Vietnam.

I've given away some of my favorite books of poetry,
    and last week I gave my favorite clear quartz
    crystal to a friend who has a new baby girl.

There's my cat, lying like a multicolored mop on the floor.
    I've had her for seventeen years, she's a treasure.

My son is a treasure, but not one that spends much time
    in the living room. He's more like mobile art,
                    on the move, with frequent stops.

Alleluia, Lord Have Mercy

As an aspiring nun (*postulant*, I was called)
my early-morning job was to scrub
the little black marks left by nuns' heels
on the rubberized tile of the long hallway of
    the Motherhouse in Kansas.
My trip began on my knees at the east
end of the hallway and ended at the west end.

At the west end were large bright sewing rooms
with shelves of black French wool serge
to be made into nuns' habits.
The sweet smell of new French wool serge
signaled the end of my morning's job.

As a nun in springtime I wore one of those long black
French wool-serge habits made in the sweet sewing room
at the hall's west end.
In my springtime, the French wool serge flowed across
the green elegant campus of my flowering nun-like
    alleluia days.

But as a nun in summertime (dog days of August in Kansas)
I wore the long wool serge habit and knelt with
five hundred other nuns, shoulder to shoulder,
(Lord have mercy) in the tiny chapel, without
air conditioning, with the sour sweet smell
of French wool serge in un-nun-like (Amen) misery.

Another Leap

The only thing I remember
from James Dickey's poem is the leap
I took as a nine-year-old from the limb
of the mesquite tree in the pasture
to the back of my roan horse

away from the house of crying
babies and clothes lines with
flapping diapers and sheets and towels
to the pasture and my nameless horse.

my leap
to the horse I rode bare-back
through the grass and cactus
holding the red mane like a bridle
my feet and legs tight against the rib cage
I rode until the horse turned too fast
threw me sliding to the ground
"the cradle endlessly rocking"
and my grandmother's voice calling.

The rock of these words
leaping from the limb on to the page as I write
my self in danger
sliding cactus words
my legs and feet reach round the cage
I can't hold on to
return to leap from one more limb
to jump one more freedom time
from the branch to the poem
riding bareback.

After the Wildfire

The poet's heart: what the fire
could not consume.
        Richard Jones

The sign says: "Do not feed the deer;
    they know how to survive, unless
    they are in shock or trauma.
Pellets and hay
    will only make them bloat and die."

These days I'm feeling disconnected,
    my dreams have stopped.
Maybe it's the flu, I don't know.
    I miss my dreams; they feed my
    poems; the poems feed my dreams.

Tonight I'm thinking about that
    mystic poet, Richard Jones.
I'd like his voice to ask the gods
    to give back my dreams
                and my poems:
Sage over my heart
        for the words;
Lavender on my forehead
        for trust;
A drop of lemon grass in the bath water
        for the poems that live
within the silence of their lines.

That's not the way Richard would
    have said it, but that's the idea.

I know how to survive:
                Do Not Feed.

At the Window

My favorite starting place is the living room,
        in the straight-backed chair
    facing the canyon and the hills in the distance.
           I sit and stare.
I'm pulled into everything in general,
        nothing in particular.

I remember how my father stood
      at the kitchen window.
        Supported by one hand on the windowsill,
      he stared into the plum orchard,
          and into the mesquite pasture and
cottonwood groves along the creek where
        the wild plums grow.

My father stood there for half an hour or who
      knows how long—all the crying babies
    and family noise behind him, he stood
        at the kitchen window.
I thought it was very strange for my father to
          stand there staring.

Today I sit staring out the window at the peach
      trees, the pasture beyond covered with lupine,
        the homes on the hillside barely visible
           through the oaks.

I stare for half an hour, or who knows how long,
    at all the wild and perfect Everything.

Separate Lives

This morning I sit alone on the living
room floor and pull a folder of old
poems from the shelf.

Some of the poems are about my son. One
is about him at age four, falling asleep during
his haircut at the Yellow Balloon.
I watch him there . . . his hair, his chin, his
eyes, his thumbs . . . all like the father
he's never met.

And the poem about him at age seven
when he explains to me the best parts
of the school play: "The little girl kicks
her legs so high with her dance that all
the boys see lots . . . and they like that,
and the part about the girls in trouble
for singing . . . *ain't no shit, with a gettin'*
like a tit, Grease Lightnin' . . . , and
the violin and fiddle music were okay."

And a poem about Paul, the Topanga neighbor,
his huge frame larger than our doorway,
asking about the holes in his truck windows
from B-B gun's missed shots.

And the daily-drive poem: out of Topanga
Canyon, breakfast sliding back
and forth on the paper plate as a I maneuver
the sharp curves getting him to school on time
and me to work early enough to grab a cup
of coffee before first period class, always
passing that line of little 12-year-old boys sitting
on the step eating free breakfasts from the school
cafeteria, all of us deserving better mothers.

Today my son leaves for Cal State, or his job, or
to teach judo or swimming, or Out, Somewehere.

Separate lives, Mom.

Collision Tears

I was involved in a collision today
    at an intersection
in Bed, Bath & Beyond. I was
coming down the main aisle
    in Sheets & Towels
and a young woman with her
    8-month-old baby boy
    pulled out of a side lane
        of Rugs & Curtains.

We collided.
Baby Boy bumped his mouth
    against the metal front of the cart.
He shrieked with pain and Mother
    picked him up, explaining to me
        that he had bumped his teething gums.
With that I started to cry
    tears as large as his
    rolling down my cheeks.

At one point we both stopped crying
    and stared at each other.
Then we started our crying all over again.
Tough, this teething, this bumping the raw
    parts of ourselves against the fierce
        metal
            carts of life.

Laundry and Death

Four loads of laundry
are swishing around in the machines
and I feel obscene opening a Tab
at this hour of the morning.
Nine o'clock on a Saturday morning,
the Tab is a reward for getting over
the hill from Topanga
to the laundromat in Woodland Hills.

Top O' Topanga the signs says
just before the descent
into the valley.
Something like Top O' the Morning.
The hills have never been greener.

I change chairs in the laundromat
because a woman in front of me
is sorting her dirty laundry.
I hate watching it—it's so real.
Real dirty laundry reminds me
too much that death comes clean
but life is nothing but dirty laundry.

All the machines are being filled
mostly by women who look just like me:
the dirty living and the clean dead.

The day I moved from Huntington Palisades
I thought I was home again
when I got to the laundromat.
All those clothes turning,
women hassling their little kids to behave.
Dogs, in and out.

The Palisades got to me, rows
upon rows of perfect homes.
The lawns perfectly manicured, silence,
curtains drawn just right,

plants always in the same place
in perfect bloom. The garage
doors always closed and the front
door always closed. Death

all so fine. Inside,
little old ladies in perfect order
in their giant mausoleums
built for themselves and they send
their garbage out once a week
in perfectly wrapped garbage bags,
sometimes in lovely red and white stripes.
All so fine and perfect.

And the local drug addict
takes his bath in the laundromat sink
and combs his hair and beard
in the reflection in the dryer door
before he walks barefoot down the street.

Bleeding Time

I see the purple bruises the size of dime on both my wrists.
My hands are wrinkled and the veins pop up with age.
I wear long-sleeved sweaters and skirts,
   and I buy one of those comfortable cotton shirt-waist dresses
   with the narrow belt.
I've become my mother.

This is not good news. I've never wanted to be my mother.
But my mother, gone now for many years, is alive in me.
I pray for a softer version of her.

When I was six I knelt at my mother's knees each night
   for night prayers: The Lord's Prayer, the Hail Mary,
   the Prayer to the Guardian Angel.

After prayers I received my mother's good night kiss,
   from lips puckered as hard as the shell of a walnut,
   pressed against my lips.
My mother's terrible goodnight kisses, hard as her life.

Her life—making patchwork quilts, window drapes,
   coats and dresses, and enough milk to feed eleven babies.

At my bathroom mirror, I examine my face, the lines bleed
   into creases above my upper lip.

The bleeding, my own solitary bleeding at 13.
"My mother didn't bleed," I speak to the mirror,
        "she had no time for bleeding."

Today I am my mother, the hard kisses,
   endless quilts and coats and dresses of my life,
   the milk that feeds and begs for time, the bleeding time.

What Is Tall and Spews Marbles

Monsignor stands in the church pulpit, his big
belly wrapped in the bright sash of his Monsignorship,
   his hands tucked under the red belt, one hand
     coming out now and then to pat his belly between
        his bellows:

        "Those evil bare legs!"

I'm six and my bare skinny legs
      feel as large and visible
as the columns down the nave of the church.

     "...those painted faces
     unworthy of communion!"

His bulging watery eyes scan the pews below.

     "...that beer, beer, beer
       and dancing, dancing, dancing,
    dancing at the Bohemian Hall.
      Hall, Hall, Hall, sin, sin, sin,
        Hell, Hell, Hell, forever
          and ever and ever and ever and ever.
      Amen."

And I faint.

Silence

Sometimes when I've talked too much
   on the phone
and I've explained enough and listened
      to feedback,
I hang up and sink into a space of silence
   that receives me like a velvet cloak
        I wrap around my naked body.

The Dead Man

He frowns when hunters kill the quail
lined on the telephone wires.
He stands at the east window
to watch the creek rise from the rain.
The hail beats down his wheat crop
and he doesn't speak.
He rides the tractor long long hours,
brings in wood for the furnace,
washes diapers and dishes.
Each morning he rises at five for oatmeal,
then milks the cows.
He maps the change of seasons
by the sun on the dining room wall
and assists at every birth,
all eleven of them.

My father is light on the inside,
dark on the outside,
so smart he lets my Mom answer all his questions,
so wise he writes only two words, his own name,
so natural he could be dumb.

He offers eleven children college educations,
but he doesn't finish sixth grade.
He buys the land that grows the wheat
to feed the cattle he takes to market.
He kneels beside his bed each night
but is depressed by churches.

Four times he speaks to me:
At eight when I burn with fever
he lays his hand on me and says,
"Feeling better?"
At sixteen he says gently,
"Listen to your mother."
At twenty, as I leave for the convent,
he says goodbye, with a tear.
At thirty-two he talks to me

about the Oklahoma Indians
at the Tulsa Art Museum.

He resoles his shoes that walk the land.
He shaves his beard with a straight-edge
sharpened on the strap.
He rolls his own.
He's a morning man who watches every sunrise.

At 86, he dies alone, though for weeks
we hover over him.
Never mind, this man knows how to die alone.

(That part of the poem is for the family—
I sent a copy to my brother Harry.
The awkward ending is the best I can do.
This part is for me.)

Were you a nice guy or not?
Speak! You never speak!
Give me something to love or hate.
Isn't there something you have to say,
something you feel?
Do I have to live out my life
wondering what you were doing in my life?
                    Pathetic man.
I didn't cry at your funeral.
At last, I was rid of being ashamed,
depressed, sorry for you. But now,
            I'm the pathetic one.
I'm afraid to say anything hateful about you,
afraid if I say something about one man,
I'll say it about all men.

If I say I hate you, even if I whisper it,
that whisper might turn into a yell,
then a scream. And I'll just go on
yelling and screaming and yelling
and screaming and yelling.
                      A pathetic yelling
screaming bitch of a woman.

Forgive me, Daddy, for screaming.
I understand your pain.
I know the part of you that got sealed
with your mother's grave at five.
These tears are mine, ones I sealed up
long before your funeral.
They are my grief
for the dead man I lived with all my life.

The Familiar Red

I'm thinking of my hometown this evening.
   I seldom do that anymore.
It started when I went to Salt Lake City.

I met Steve at his art studio
in the Salt Lake City Art Center.
After exchanging small talk, I discovered
Steve is one of the few people I've met
who has been to my hometown:
   Okarche, Oklahoma, population 500.
The sign hasn't changed since I was a child.

Turns out Steve delivered refrigerators
to Okarche on his first job.

We talked about Oklahoma, the red dirt,
the red sunsets from all the red dust
in the air, and what it was like for him
to have gone from delivering refrigerators
   to having his own studio
in the Salt Lake City Art Center.

Steve invited me to spend time at the studio
   on a day he was doing a firing.
He gave me a glob of clay to play with.
I kneaded the clay to get the bubbles out and
   and then divided it into two portions.

I didn't have any idea what to make.
I molded one part of the clay
into a bird's nest with three baby birds in it,
   their beaks wide open waiting for food.
One baby bird had a worm hanging
       out of its beak.

I molded the other piece of clay
into a loaf of bread (that was easy)
and I carved into the top, "Okarche's Finest Bread."

Okarche, my hometown.

My mother bent over the bread pan,
  baking bread for her eleven baby birds.

Weird Waltzing

And now my life is in place,
and I wonder about the two dreams.

I know both of those women:
the one dancing with the man;
and the one walking alone,
reaching out to the woman ahead of her,

The first dream is a dance to the Tennessee Waltz.
    The man says the last dance is for me.
The dance is right; they move across the large floor
    melding together to the Tennessee Waltz.

The second dream is a walk to the Tennessee Waltz.
The woman on a wooded trail wears only
the pants of her jogging suit, her arms crossing the lower
    part of her breasts, covering her nipples.
She is singing the Tennessee Waltz,
tears forming on the words as she reaches out
      to the woman ahead of her.

Motion

Zanzibar

In Zanzibar, at the hotel, a scene plays before my eyes. It's a Muslim world; I sit alone, a blond woman, unveiled, on a bar stool, of the dim hotel after sundown. Hunger gnaws at my stomach; I clutch my handbag for my wallet.

But, wait, this poem should have mystery and even romance. Zanzibar has silversmiths, yes, with dark eyes, and the scent of clove. And there are caverns, or at least suggestions of them, in streets, narrow and winding. And dim shops filled with cedar trunks with silver latches, in Zanzibar.

I'm the lone woman at the hotel bar. A man turns towards me; my smile betrays my discomfort, but what can I do. I smile and he smiles. No, I say, I'm not the woman for Room 39. No, and I move to a side table, less visible, I think. But others watch me, and again, "No, I'm not the woman for Room 39." I look down and away from their gazes. I walk to the front lobby, as confidently as an unveiled woman in Zanzibar can. Only my hunger has brought me out after sundown, guided by a young boy through the dark winding streets from the hostel to this hotel.

The island doctor in the front lobby is the first to speak; he invites me to dinner. He says he sees my discomfort. At the candlelit dinner he has stories: history, his etchings, his seashells. And then the question.

"Not tonight," I say, "but maybe tomorrow, or some day." (If a woman is kind, will he hear her?) After dinner the doctor escorts me to the Chief of Police; turns me over to him, with trust I think.

The Chief of Police drives me down long dirt roads to the opposite tip of the island, within view of small motel rooms, and says, "We could stop here."

"Please," I say, "it has been a long day." Then the long dark drive back to the hostel.

But how does the Chief of Police end the story today? For his own sake, I hope he tells of a young woman, "more wildcat than woman," who leaps from his car within a block of her room and disappears wild-eyed and shimmering into the night.

Or of a young woman, who, gliding on the light of weaver-bird wings, flies away to the top frond of a coconut palm. After all, life is not all pain and logic. No one would live for that. I mean, Zanzibar is about romance and mystery, the dark eyes of silversmiths, shops of cedar trunks and silver linings, tall slender coconut palms, and the deep rich scent of clove—and women.

Oatmeal

It's five A.M. on the farm in Okarche, Oklahoma. My father sits with his bowl of oatmeal at the kitchen table. The kitchen doors are closed; the heat from the stove warms the room. My father is alone, the only time of day he is alone. In the four bedrooms upstairs on double beds, single beds and cots my ten brothers and sisters are still sleeping. My mother sleeps until seven in the downstairs bedroom. My father's daily routine is to cook thick, sticky oatmeal and brew a pot of strong coffee for his breakfast.

Today I treat myself to breakfast with my father. I'm not interested in mushy, slimy oatmeal, but if it means time with my father, I will eat oatmeal. He has a look of surprise on his serious face as I open the door to the warm kitchen and seat my bony eight-year-old body at the opposite end of the rectangular table. He scoops warm oatmeal from the cooking pot into my bowl and serves me, letting me add cream and sugar to the mix. In the morning warmth and quiet of dawn we eat oatmeal. My father eats with is left hand and sits with his legs crossed, his bald head bent forward. We glance at each other between bites and make small talk.

"Did you sleep well?"

"Yes, the wind didn't wake me."

The wind kept me awake in the dustbowl days of the '30s in Oklahoma.

I tell my father it's good to be up early, and that I like the warm kitchen, and then we are quiet again with our oatmeal. Even at age eight, I know he believes in oatmeal the way some people believe in God or exercise.

My father is a hard-working farmer, and I know that 5 A.M. is my only chance to experience what I consider to be the best of him, this quiet comfort and the breakfast experience in the warm kitchen.

Today, decades later at seven A.M., my husband is still sleeping and I am eating oatmeal, alone, feeling good about the primal experience of this slimy mix. I'm reading Galway Kinnel's poem "Oatmeal."

Galway says he is aware it is not good to eat oatmeal alone, not good for mental health. So, he invites imaginary companions such as John Keats or Edmund Spenser or John Milton to share oatmeal. They recite their poems: "To Autumn" or "Ode to a Nightingale."

Today I share my oatmeal with Galway Kinnel and together we recite "Oatmeal" to honor my father for his days alone in the warm womb of the kitchen.

Who knows, maybe my father shared oatmeal with an imaginary Mother (the mother who died when he was three) the same way Kinnel shared oatmeal with Keats. Who knows, maybe over their oatmeal my father and his imaginary mother sang lullabies—Brahms lullabies so beautiful they made the sun rise.

Divine Intervention

I had a dream. In the dream a handsome man with dark eyes and dark hair, an American Indian, appeared. He was gentle and his message was that he was there to help me. I was turning sixty-five and was twenty pounds overweight. I was curious and confused when I awoke from the dream. In the ensuing days I told several women friends about the dream.

On a windy day a week or two later, I walked down Wilshire Boulevard to Seattle's Best coffee shop and stood in line with everyone. I noticed I was standing behind a man who was an obvious body builder. "Where do you work out?" I asked. I assumed I was talking with someone who worked out at a gym. Instead, I was talking with Elio, the owner of Elio's gym at the corner of Wilshire and Centinela, a block away.

I ordered my coffee and a bagel and with my LA Times went to a table in the corner. Soon Elio appeared and said, "Can we continue our conversation?" When he sat across from me, I noticed he was the man from my dream. "You are the man from my dream," I said, "Except that the man from my dream was Indian."

"I'm Peruvian, land of the Incas and Macchu Picchu, is that Indian enough for you?"

Whoa! I told Elio that the man in my dream said he was there to help me. Elio didn't listen too much to that; instead he was fascinated that we were dressed alike in light blue sweatshirts, black tights, white shoes and socks, and each wore a touch of red.

Over our morning coffee, we shared about our lives. I told him about the large family I grew up with in Oklahoma and about my fifteen years in the convent. He interrupted just long enough to ask about my first sex after all those years. "Good," I said and continued about my years in the Peace Corps and the years raising my son as a single parent. Elio told me about being raised by his mother in Peru and about being chosen Mr. Lima, before leaving Peru for the USA to work in the field of fitness. Elio invited me to his gym and offered forty-five minutes of free treadmill. I walked three miles on the treadmill that day and each succeeding day, and lost the extra weight.

As I left the gym that first day, Elio reminded me that our relationship was spiritual. All I knew was that the gentle man with the dark eyes, dark hair, and the Inca smile got me to the gym every day. I call it Divine Intervention.

Everyone Should Have a Chance

It was the third year of teaching in Topeka, Kansas. I had seventy-five sixth graders in a makeshift room in the gym. Our voices echoed form the high ceiling, up the hallways, to other classrooms, and into the principal's office. After one semester of classes in the gym, a new classroom was completed and all seventy-five of us moved into our new location, still not quite adequate for seventy-five. We were a cozy group.

Sixth graders, at least the sixth graders of the '50s, loved working together on projects. They were proud of their group accomplishments, and I used every skill I could muster as a motivator. I was a Sister of Charity at the time, wearing the traditional long French wool habit, complete with coif, starched headband and collar, and a black veil attached to a starched linen headdress.

One spring day some of the sixth graders had a great idea and went to the principal's office for her support and approval. It was to be a surprise. At 2:30 one afternoon in May, the principal called my classroom asking for six of the pupils to come to the office.

They went and returned with a crown of fresh flowers. As they opened the classroom door, all the students began singing the song they had written for me as Queen of the May. One of the students came forward to put the flowers on my head (forgetting that a crown of flowers wouldn't work on top of black serge and a starched linen headdress). I came to the rescue and took the flowers in my hands.

Not everything about teaching was as pleasant as the year I taught the seventy-five sixth graders in the overcrowded classroom. I was nervous my very first day of teaching. It was a class of fifty-five sixth graders. For starters, they were all disappointed to have lost their former fifth grade teacher whom they loved and wanted back.

I had been told that it was important to establish good discipline the first day in the classroom, then students wouldn't take advantage of my inexperience. I heard that. So, that first day the school bell rang, and all the students took their assigned seats, in alphabetical order, so I could remember their names. As I finished taking roll call, one of the girls came to my desk to ask if she could please go to the restroom. I hesitated to answer her lest she be one of those taking advantage of a new teacher. But before I could answer, she vomited all over my desk and the floor. All the students hurried to help with the cleanup and we were off to a wonderful year together.

Effortless

Effortless, as in Esther Williams' swimming in her 1940s movies. Esther, gliding through the deep blue water with perfect grace, surfacing with perfect makeup, and a perfect smile.

Effortless, as in my son Michael taking the ocean waves on his boogie board, rolling and turning like a dolphin. Effortless, as in Jim snorkeling and pretending to be a sea creature for the camera in Hawaii.

I grew up on a farm in Oklahoma, a place short on water and long on hot dry windy summer days. As kids we emptied the horse tank. We scooped out all the water and mud, and prayed to the windmill gods to fill the tank for swimming. The horse tank, made of brick and cement, 8'x22', with a depth of 2½', was our swimming pool. We spent hours in it. There I first fantasized that I could glide through the water with a smile like Esther Williams.

I always wanted to be Esther. When I was sixteen, I visited my friend Ann Buck on her ranch in Tucumcari, New Mexico. She took me to the municipal pool which had the highest diving board I had ever seen. I visualized myself as Esther, entering the blue pool water from the high board. But somewhere between take-off and entry, a malfunction caused me to land flat on the surface of the water with an explosive pop. For weeks Esther wore ugly purple bruises.

In college a sign was posted in the P.E. department for volunteers for a water ballet. That spelled grace and beauty to me, so I signed my name. Each morning we met at the pool at 6 A.M. for an hour and practiced for the ballet. We did the back stroke, the front dolphin, back dolphin, side stroke, treading water, but we didn't ever practice the entire show. I found swimming hard, and when the instructor wasn't watching, I grabbed the side of the pool for rest.

The big night arrived, and there were flood lights, and swimming music—the Blue Danube, I think—and a crowd of spectators. There was no faking it. The flood lights caught me grabbing the side of the pool for rest and walking on the floor of the pool near the shallow end while still moving my arms in a swim stroke. I went directly to the dressing room after the performance. No movie star's star on my dressing room door.

Today for a water experience, I go to the mineral waters at Sycamore Springs on a full moon night. Jim and I climb the stairs to reach the highest tub. He takes my hand and leads me into the warm waters. For an hour we sit on benches in the tub and I stare at the full moon shining through the oak trees, just like Esther.

Push, Glide, Glide

As a seven-year-old I believed I was well on my way to becoming a champion roller skater. I had all the physical qualities of a champion: speed, poise, agility. I had a skater's body, too; it offered little wind resistance. On a good day I weighed about forty pounds. "Bones," my sister Lucy called me.

My skating rink was the cement rectangular porch about eight feet by thirty feet on the north side of our farm home. The porch was where I practiced my skating glides, glides that took me from one end of the porch to the other. I specialized in glides because I had only one skate. My workout went something like this: Initial push-off at the tall arbor vitae at the east end of the porch, and a glide (arms outstretched) to the low-lying junipers at the west end of the porch, all without touching the skateless foot to the porch, the latter skill a definite sign of a pro. Practice, practice, practice. I loved it; I had all the will and endurance of a winner.

But I had no skate key. It was lost with the other skate years before I arrived on the scene. That did not deter me. I had state-of-the-art leather straps for my heels and ankles and some quart-sized canning jar rubbers holding my skinny toes to the metal of the skate.

I skated for hours those summer afternoons, gliding from one end of the porch to the other, maneuvering the perpendicular crack in the center with grace and aplomb. I pushed the stringy blond hair out of my blue eyes and waved to my appreciative audience: the dog, the baby guineas, and the goslings feeding on the Bermuda grass in the large fenced yard. Sometimes I looked through the storm windows, into the living and dining room, towards my mother at the sewing machine, but she didn't look back. Everyone in the large family was doing his own thing on the large farm. My thing this summer was skating. I was a champion: Push, glide, glide, glide, push, wave, wave . . .

The Toy Shop

Not every eight-year-old farm girl thinks of her grandfather's blacksmith shop as a toy shop. I did.

After my grandfather's death at our farm home in Oklahoma, the old blacksmith shop with all the tools and equipment for making bridles and harnesses and horseshoes was abandoned in the name of technical progress.

I loved the blacksmith shop with its smell of leather and oil. On summer days the shop was a cool place with its wide cracks in the walls and no door to stop a constant cross breeze.

The blacksmith shop faced south. To the left of the doorway was a long work table, almost the length of the shop. This table held the vice and hammers, files, levelers, gauges, nails, tacks and every kind of tool for hole punching and leather cutting. On the wall above the table was the array of small tools for harness-making.

On the opposite side of the blacksmith shop was a large circular cement-and-iron firing tank with bellows, and an anvil and large prongs to hold hot pieces for making or repairing horseshoes, and hoes, and cultivator parts. Large saws and scythes hung from this side of the shop.

Under a shelf in the northwest corner of the shop, two geese sat on their nests, waiting for their eggs to hatch. Sometimes I helped the goslings out of their shells if I thought they were having trouble breaking out.

Now and then squirrels came to visit, but they didn't stay.

During our summers my brother Harry and I built stilts and go-carts, slingshots, and whatever else we could dream up. The blacksmith shop was ours to enjoy. We tried all the saws, drills, bits, gauges and leather punches, all my grandfather's priceless tools.

All those priceless tools, necessary for his survival, now the summer toys in the hands of Grandpa George's grandchildren.

Large Talents

This morning as I whip up a batch of buckwheat cookies before breakfast, I think of my mother. She often baked before breakfast. As I observe my thin arms stirring the batter, I think for a moment, I am my mother, now dead for fifteen years.

My mother baked six or eight loaves of bread twice a week and every day she baked either cookies or cakes for school lunches, at one point eight school lunches. I liked the aroma of fresh baking when I walked into the house at the end of the school day. For my mother, fixing school lunches for eleven children spanned a period of about twenty years.

I didn't appreciate my mother when I was in elementary school. I didn't like the way my lunches looked—those bulky homemade sandwiches with their farm steak and the homemade cookies and cakes that weren't perfectly shaped. I didn't like them. I wanted Wonder Bread sandwiches and perfect chocolate-marshmallow store cookies that my friends had. I wanted a pretty lunch, not a homemade lunch.

My mother cooked and canned everything from fruits and vegetables to mincemeat pies. Everything was homegrown and homemade and stored in Mason jars. Everything I wore was homemade, too; sometimes even my skin felt stitched by my mother. After the Great Depression, she sewed dresses from printed flour sacks. If one sack didn't make a complete dress, she improvised with islet trim and lace ruffles. She made all the drapes in the house and all the patchwork quilts and comforters on the beds. She made soap for laundering and starched and ironed all shirts, dresses and tablecloths. There were no plastics in our home. In Okarche everything was fine and "starchy."

My mother embroidered, crocheted and knitted. More than that, she was a homework specialist. Every evening when the dinner table was cleared of dishes (my father helped with dishes in the evening) the homework came out, under my mother's guidance and supervision. She knew fractions and grammar and literature. When I was twelve I won a price for a poem. I know my mother helped me write it because the poem contained the word "dearth."

As far as I can remember there were only two things my mother did poorly: algebra and driving.

As I grew up I don't ever remember my mother saying she was tired. Her greatest joy was having all her children for Sunday meals, all home-cooked, of course. The family got very large as it began to include sons- and daughters-in-law and grandchildren. An intimate family dinner now included seventy people.

When my mother was ninety-three and a little senile, she was rummaging through the closet one night at 3:00 A.M. I asked what she was doing and she said she was looking for extra blankets for the babies who were cold. Even at ninety-three there were still chores.

Country Culture

A part of me believes I grew up culturally disadvantaged.

On our farm in central Oklahoma we didn't have access to books, or art, and access to music was minimal. We had a piano in the sunroom, but several keys above middle C didn't work, and the piano needed tuning. I took piano lessons for about six months from Sister Virgila at Holy Trinity and from her and from a music appreciation class, I learned to read music.

Any appreciation of music came from my mother's side of the family. Her two older sisters, Aunt Margaret and Aunt Loretta, both gave piano lessons in the community, and both of these aunts played well. My mother played when she had time, but the old untuned piano was a problem. Even so, I loved it when my mother sat at the piano and played and sang.

However, at Holy Trinity Parish, it was a different scene. The church had a pipe organ with a most extensive set of pipes. Every Sunday morning at the 10 o'clock High Mass, Kate Heinen, the organist, pulled out all the stops, and the German choir sang the Latin Mass and Latin hymns in all their full-throated polyphonic harmonies. Church pews vibrated with the intensity of the sound, and with the addition of incense and candles, I sometimes fainted.

As a child, I remember turning around during the services to look up into the choir loft at Kate Heinen playing the pipe organ. She was tough, yanking up her skirts and spreading her legs to get full access to the foot pedals. She bounced from one end of the organ bench to the other as she reached for the varying levels of organ keys and pedals.

For the early Sunday Masses, the grade school children usually sang hymns; only the 10 A.M. High Mass featured the German Choir with pipe organ accompaniment by Kate Heinen.

I returned to Holy Trinity church a few years ago for my sister's funeral; I saw that the pipe organ and all the pipes had been removed, and there stood a small electric organ, and the choir was composed of one female soloist. Modern simplicity replaced the

German choir. Gone also were the days of chanting long litanies in Latin with the priest singing the petition, and the choir answering with a refrain such as *terragamos audinos*. As a young child I thought I heard in that refrain something about a "snotty nose."

Full Circle

It was the winter of '68. I had just left the convent in Kansas after fifteen years as a Sister of Charity; I arrived at UCLA with a brief case containing all my "worldly possessions," and I stared my new job in graduate admissions in the Department of Psychology. It felt strange because I had no frame of reference for functioning in a world outside the convent. Entering the Peace Corps was the last thing on my mind.

At UCLA I lived in the apartment complex across the street from the Botanical Gardens, two blocks from work. The psychology professors were understanding of me and offhandedly remarked, "Welcome to the human race." I tried to keep my inexperience hidden, but I was being asked what salary I wanted while I was still adjusting to the price of a loaf of bread.

It was 1968, the year I entered the Peace Corps. Fate arranged it. Each morning before 8 A.M. a Persian student burst out the front door of his apartment, and from the balcony would sing "Born Free," just those two words in full voice every morning; then he ran down the three flights of stairs and was off to engineering school for the day.

One spring day the Persian student stopped me at the mailbox. He handed me an envelope explaining that he's not American citizen, so why would they send this to him. He handed me a Peace Corps application.

I took the application, filled it out and mailed it in. It was a good idea from the start. I was searching for something, it was obvious. A behavioral psychologist had commented on it when I changed from wearing conservative suits to wearing min-skirts and boots, and sometimes a full light-brown natural hair wig. One of the women in the office gave me a silk jersey magenta mini-dress, which I chose to wear with my natural wig and boots to Louisiana to enter Peace Corps training. I left UCLA in mid-October.

Peace Corps training in Louisiana was no picnic: the site was a vacant summer camp for underprivileged boys. When we arrived it was not summer, although that first night it was still hot at 11 P.M. On arrival at the camp we built our beds from the frames and mattresses that were stacked in the corners of the cabins. There were no glass panes on the windows, we had no hot water, and some time during that first night the temperature dropped to near freezing. It began to rain and it rained every day until December. For warmth I slept with a mattress under me and another one on top for a blanket.

I arrived at the summer camp wearing my natural hair wig, my magenta silk jersey dress and leather boots. The following morning over hominy grits in the dining hall, I heard people asking about "the woman." Where had she gone? I explained where she had gone and that she was now in Peace Corps training.

The first day we fifty volunteers met our African language and cultural studies instructors and the training began. As it was cold and uncomfortable to sleep at night, we set up a canteen and danced and sang to Beatles tapes until very late . . . "Remember to let her into heart, and you can start to make it better. Hey Jude . . . " In December we flew (sleep deprived) to Malawi, East Africa, for our Peace Corps service.

Life in Africa was much easier than the summer camp in Louisiana. After more language study and orientation we were sent to our posts. Mine was a little village named Malindi, separated from the rest of the country by the Shire River and Lake Malawi. It was a remote section of the country accessible only by ferry boat across the Shire River. Wild game was protected here, and this was the area where the revolutionary, Henry Chipembere, had lived at the time of his failed coup d'etat.

All my language training was of no benefit here because the people of Malindi spoke not a Bantu dialect but Yao. However, there wasn't much speaking going on. These villagers were friends and family of Henry Chipembere, and for their safety they chose to speak very little and quietly.

My Peace Corps assignment at the Malindi Teacher Training College was to teach English to the men and prepare them to be elementary school teachers. The students came from various parts of Malawi, boarded at the college, and had varying levels of English fluency. I could not tell how much of my English, with my American Midwestern accent, they understood.

Life was basic in Malindi. Electricity was limited to an hour or two from a generator in the evening. Gecko-watching was a favorite form of evening entertainment. With help from the village people, we teachers boiled and filtered our water, and ironed our clothes to kill flukes carried in the water. Two British VSO teachers shared the living space with Peggy, Peace Corps volunteer, and me. I read all the books provided in the Peace Corps paperback library.

Within a few months of being in Malindi, I realized the real reason I was in this small village in East Africa. It wasn't about giving the students American ideas. It was a two-way learning experience. In the classroom, as I mentioned, I was never quite sure the men understood me. The English they knew, they had learned from the British, with a British accent. The men were reserved and polite, and I began to realize I was probably getting much more than I was giving.

I especially liked what I was receiving from the village people. They were in tune with nature; I loved the sounds. The fishermen fished all night on the lake and sang messages to other fishing boats. The villagers drummed messages of weddings, new babies, or approaching danger. They knew the hippos, the hyenas, the elephants. They danced and they sang and they worked. All of my previous convent rigidity, with the dogma, and doctrine, and competition fell away. I was living in a thatched home feeling secure under my mosquito net at night, listening to dozens of sounds I couldn't identify. I soon learned the sounds of snorting hippos in the vegetable gardens on the lake shore.

There were no cars (only an occasional lorry), no phones, no TV, no lights, no signs, no commercial buildings. There were only the small thatched huts, the teacher training college buildings and the small medical clinic. And, of course, the wide lake with its delicious chombo fish, and tall vegetation, and giant ant hills.

Malawi was healing. This slow walk with people who were quiet, people whose language I couldn't speak, this walk down trails through the tall grass along the seashore, down non-roads, gave back the gift of my life I thought I had lost.

That was my first year in Malindi which included going into even more remote areas to supervise the men's student teaching.

And then a turn of events led to my moving to the capital city of Blantyre to work for the Peace Corps Director and the Medical Staff. Ed Larsh, the Director, explained in a newsletter to the volunteers that his secretary had completed her two-year term and was returning the United States. He was now without a secretary and office help. He needed help.

This was also a time when a large Scottish mercenary who worked for President Kamuzu Banda was spending time roaming around at night with his machine gun, tracking down Chipembere sympathizers in the village. The mercenary would announce his presence at my door by casually slipping his machine gun from his shoulder and slinging it across the cement floor. He was the reason the villagers were silent; their safety and their lives depended on it.

And there was Roberto, the Italian ex-priest, who was married to the Canadian village doctor. Roberto taught biology at the teacher training college. Between classes Roberto took to pursuing me, and once at night appeared at my bedroom window calling to me, pushing a long stick through the louvered window into my mosquito net. Roberto from passionate Italy . . .

I wrote Ed Larsh and asked to work for him. The reason I gave was not the truth. I told him there was not enough work for me in Malindi. I explained that I was accustomed to working long hours every day as a Sister of Charity. I didn't ever tell him about Don the mercenary or Roberto the biology teacher.

Life in Blantyre was completely different from Malindi. I worked six days a week in the Peace Corps office for the Director, the Medical Staff, and conducted business with the American Embassy involving Peace Corps volunteers. When the volunteers came in from their villages for supplies or medical help, I took time to give them haircuts, if wanted, and maybe even gave them space on my floor for overnight keep.

Peace Corps volunteers were close friends. We hitchhiked great distances to be together on traditional American holidays. Hitch-hiking wasn't easy. However, Europeans didn't like to see us on the road, so they would offer lifts. I remember that Fran Reid and I hitchhiked to spend Thanksgiving with Peace Corps friends in Ncheu, seventy miles away. It was quite a challenge to hitch-hike carrying a live turkey, our contribution to the upcoming Thanksgiving dinner.

Every day in Malawi brought new experiences, so the stories go on and on. The people of Malawi were the great gift; they were examples of gentleness, kindness, and simplicity in their lives. They had such beauty in their singing, drumming, and dancing, and even their handshakes were gestures of amazing sensitivity. Their lives were difficult but honest and beautiful.

After two years in Malawi, I returned to the United States. I came full circle back to UCLA, this time to the Vice-Chancellor's office. The Persian student, who sang "Born Free" every morning and had given me the Peace Corps application, was gone. But, as fate would have it, within a few days after my return, I met an Israeli woman I had known two years earlier in the Department of Psychology. She had been to Zambia and, when she learned I had been to Malawi, asked if I would like to meet Henry Chipembere. Henry Chipembere! I supposed he was dead. A few days later I did meet Henry Chipembere. I had been in his village of Malindi, so I was like family to him. He took my hand in his in the traditional Malawian greeting—slow, moving. I had thought Henry Chipembere was dead because he was diabetic, and I had heard that his insulin supply was cut off when he was trying to escape. But here he was in Los Angeles. Henry Chipembere warned me not to write to Malawi about him, so that no harm would come to his family and friends.

At the time of my meeting Henry Chipembere, he was assigned to teach a course through the California State University system. His course, which I took, was Contemporary East African Politics. The class met in a home in Baldwin Hills. What a gift to be in a class where the teacher knew personally all the leaders of the East African countries. I was honored to be in Henry Chipembere's presence.

Today when I open my mailbox and find a Peace Corps Malawi Newsletter, I realize a large piece of my heart is still in Africa.

Topanga

The part of Los Angeles I call home is Topanga, where I lived for fourteen years. In 1979 I did not plan to leave Venice to live in Topanga, but my rental home on Amoroso Court went for sale, and my seven-year-old son and I needed a new place to live. (Venice had been fun with the beach and boardwalk jugglers and musicians, and Beyond Baroque with its poets and poetry readings) I received a lucky tip about a rental in Topanga; I took it sight unseen.

That is how my son and I came to live in a converted horse stable, surrounded by large oaks, two blocks from 8,000 acres of State Park in the Santa Monica Mountains. I adopted hiking as my favorite free sport and began to experience what is called the energy of Topanga. Every day on my way home from work at John Adams Jr. High, I turned off Pacific Coast Highway and took a deep breath to feel the peace of the Canyon as I drove the four miles on Topanga Canyon Boulevard into Topanga.

Topanga is not about the city. Topanga is little more than a market, a post office, coffee shops, a lumber yard, and the Inn of the Seventh Ray; however, a mile further into Canyon on the creek side is the famous Will Geer outdoor theater where I saw *A Midsummer's Nights Dream* and *As You Like It*, among other performances. Beyond the Will Geer and up the winding hill to the right is the Community House where I saw the *Nutcracker* performed every year with all-Topanga talent.

The best part of Topanga is always the hiking. It became my way of life and a source of entertainment and exploration for my son and his friend Nick. I knew every rock and trail in the large park. Today I have two deer and coyote jawbones, teeth intact, that Michael and Nick gave me as gifts from their hiking excursions in the State Park when they were ten years old.

At various times I hiked with friends, but hiking partners were not necessary for me. Sometimes groups of us participated in Solstice celebrations at a huge rock formation we called Eagle Rock.

These celebrations had accompanying drumming and chanting and were at night.

Today when I return to Topanga, I discover bumper to bumper traffic through the Canyon, overflow from the 101 Freeway. I see mansionizers carving out the hillsides. I have to remember what the Topanga writer Carolyn See said, "These hills are large enough to accommodate all; don't worry." Now, as I wend my way through the Canyon from Atascadero, I see the familiar chiseled rock profiles I call the Indian Canyon Protectors. I see the giant Turtle Rock, and the 50-foot Phallic Rock. The Canyon always accommodates me.

And Then One Day

By 1997 I was settled as a single woman in Santa Monica, my son was fully self-supporting, and my massage business was providing a perfect retirement income.

But life has a way of intruding on plans. One day my friend Zo and I were having morning coffee at a table outside Mort's Deli in Pacific Palisades. As we talked, I saw a man coming up the sidewalk; I noticed that he had what I describe as flying energy. He gestured hello and flew by, a man with a mission. Throughout the summer of '97 I kept encountering this man. With each of our accidental meetings I could see that he was getting interested in me. I didn't think we were a match.

And then one evening I was participating in a small discussion group in Pacific Palisades. Flying Man was part of the group; everyone was laughing and happy—everyone but me, that is.

At one point during the meeting, I took time to close my eyes to go inward. With my eyes closed, I asked myself what kind of woman I wanted to be: the sad, withdrawn one I was being or a happy, laughing one like the others. I decided on happy over sad, and as I opened my eyes I looked directly into the eyes of Flying Man, Jim Cone, seated across from me. Instinctively I said to myself: What's not to like about this man?

We were married October 16, 1999 in Topanga under the oak trees, in the backyard, overlooking the deep canyon; surrounded by dozens of happy relatives and friends sharing our joy.

Jim, Flying Man, owned a small plane and had flown for many years as a commercial airline pilot. Suddenly life ratcheted up several notches as we were flying to Mexico with Flying Samaritans, the Grand Canyon, Catalina Island, Oregon, and to and from Los Angeles from the Central Coast.

Today in Atascadero, plane or no plane, retirement is beautiful as the flying spirit still soars in the lives of The Pilot and the Nun.

www.ingramcontent.com/pod-product-compliance
Lightning Source LLC
Chambersburg PA
CBHW060502110426
42738CB00055B/2589